The true and living God is the creator and ruler of all things.

Object: lump of clay, package of dust

God created all things. His creation proves He is the Creator.

Start with a lump of clay. Read with the children Isaiah 64:8.

Form a little animal from the clay. It can be very simple, showing our meager ability to form something of value from clay. Ask a child to come up and hold the animal.

Can you make him wag his tail? Can you make him walk? God did. He created all the animals and put life into them.

God made each of us. But He didn't use

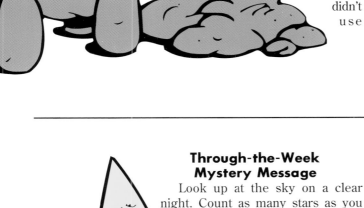

clay. *(Show bag of dust.)* Could you make a person out of this dust? No. But God did. He made the first man from dust. Then He breathed His own breath into him God is the one who causes each one of us to receive life.

We believe God is the Creator because we can see that only He could make this wonderful world and the people in it. God tells us this in the book He has given us. Genesis 1:1—"In the beginning God created the heavens and the earth."

Additional object: a large mum

Take a large mum and show how as many as 150 petals are put together to form this beautiful flower.

Only God could make such a lovely flower grow from a tiny seed. He is the giver of life.

Through-the-Week Mystery Message

Look up at the sky on a clear night. Count as many stars as you can. Remember, there are millions more you cannot see! What does the sky tell you about God? Think of three things. Write them on this star and bring it to class next week.

Suggested facts: (1) God carefully designed the heavens so that each star has its place. (2) God is able to keep each part of the heavens in its place. (3) God is powerful. (4) God is intelligent. (5) God loves us and provides just what we need to live on this earth.

Provide a star made of yellow construction paper and the words "What the sky tells me about God" on top point. Offer a small prize for each one who brings his star back with at least one thing written on it. —M.E.

Craft 1

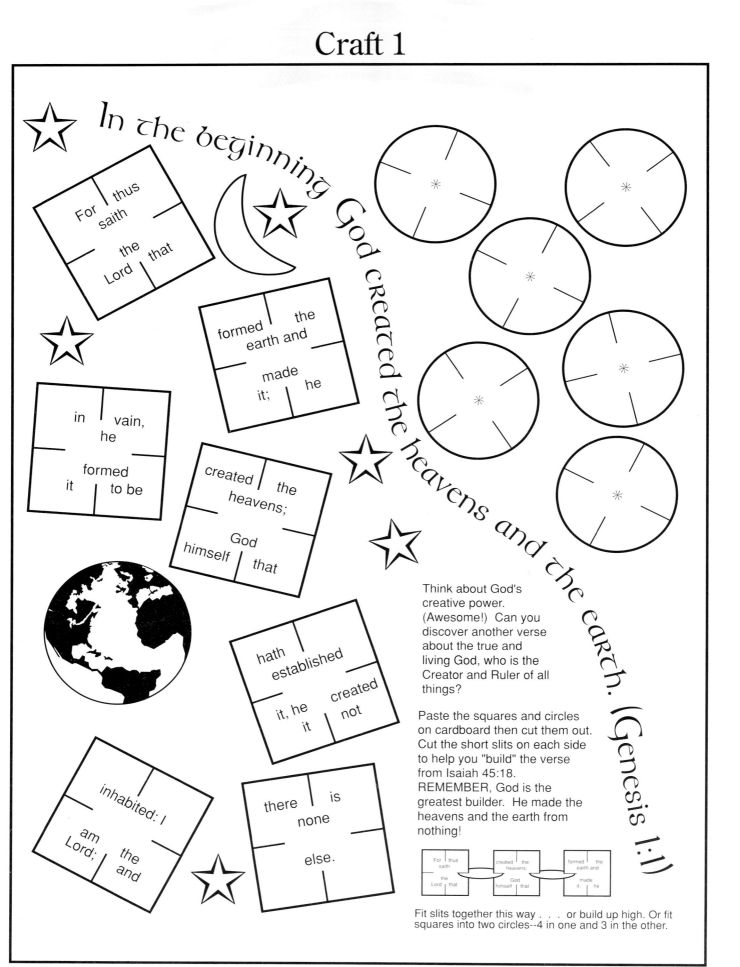

In the beginning God created the heavens and the earth. (Genesis 1:1)

For thus saith the Lord that

formed the earth and made it; he

in vain, he formed it to be

created the heavens; God himself that

hath established it, he created it not

inhabited: I am Lord; the and

there is none else.

Think about God's creative power. (Awesome!) Can you discover another verse about the true and living God, who is the Creator and Ruler of all things?

Paste the squares and circles on cardboard then cut them out. Cut the short slits on each side to help you "build" the verse from Isaiah 45:18. REMEMBER, God is the greatest builder. He made the heavens and the earth from nothing!

Fit slits together this way . . . or build up high. Or fit squares into two circles--4 in one and 3 in the other.

The Lord Jesus Christ is God's only perfect Son.

Objects: a small dinner roll and paper plate

As you talk about the miracle of the feeding of the 5,000, slowly tear apart the dinner roll into very small pieces.

One day the people Jesus taught became very hungry. Because He loved them and wanted them to know who He really was, He decided to feed them. There were over 5,000 people!

A little boy willingly gave his lunch of five rolls and two fish to Jesus. I have one roll here today. If the boy had five rolls and there was 5,000 people, how many people would one roll have to feed? Right—1,000!

Well, let's see, do you think I have broken this roll into 1,000 pieces? *Maybe* I could get 1,000 *crumbs* if I worked long enough! But wait! Let's see what the Bible says. "When they were *filled*"—The people didn't receive only a crumb. Their stomachs were filled. And more than that. There were 12 baskets of leftovers! What a miracle that was.

Maybe someone might say, "But there were also two fish in the boy's lunch." Now they would have needed to be humongous fish to feed all those people! Besides that, the Bible says right here—two *small* fish.

There is only one person in all the universe who could feed 5,000 people with five loaves and two small fish. Do you know who it is? Yes. The true and living God who made us. Jesus is indeed the Son of God.

God Himself spoke from Heaven one day and said, "This is my beloved Son in whom I am well pleased." *The Lord Jesus Christ is God's only perfect Son.*

Through-the-Week Mystery Message

Find a seed this week. It could be in an apple, a grape or other fruit. It may be a seed from a tree or a flower. How does this seed remind you of the miracle Jesus did? Think of two things. Write them on this apple and bring it to class next week.

(1) He used something very little to do a big miracle. (2) God is the one who makes the seed grow. (3) From that one tiny seed can come many more trees, with more fruit and more seeds.

Provide an apple made of red construction paper and the words "how the seed reminds me of Jesus' miracle." Offer a small prize for each one who brings the apple back with at least one thing written on it. —M.E.

how the seed reminds me of Jesus' miracle

The Lord Jesus Christ is God the Father's only perfect Son!

Just think, when you receive Jesus as your Savior – **You are a child of the King!**

800 years ago in England and France knights used a coat of arms to show others who they were. Make your own "God's Family" coat of arms by thinking about the important facts above.

1. Include John 3:16 or John 1:1 in one section.
2. Draw a picture of how life began on earth for the Son of God.
3. Draw a picture of something good about your being in God's family.
4. Draw a picture in the last section showing the "special book" God's family uses.

You can hang this small coat of arms on your bulletin board or maybe you will want to make a large one from cardboard!

The Holy Spirit is the Spirit of God.

Object: A gold circle (plain bracelet or ring)

As we learn what a Christian believes, we are using an object to help us remember each belief.

This gold circle reminds me of the Holy Spirit.

The circle has no beginning or end. God has no beginning or ending. He has always lived. He is eternal. Because the Holy Spirit is the Spirit of God He is eternal. He has no beginning or end.

The Bible also calls Him the Spirit of Christ. That is because God the Father, God the Son and God the Holy Spirit are one God. Sometimes we call our God the Trinity, which means three in one. We cannot explain our great and mighty three-in-one God. But we can believe what God tells us in the Bible.

Although we cannot see the Holy Spirit we can see what He does in the life of a Christian. When a person receives Jesus as his Savior the Holy Spirit begins to change that person. We can see that he becomes more and more like the Lord Jesus as he obeys God.

There are two special verses we want to look at that tell about our three-in-one God.

In John 14:26 Jesus said, "The Holy Ghost, whom the father will send in my name, he shall teach you all things and bring all things to your remembrance...." The Holy Spirit helps us understand the Bible and reminds us of God's word.

This next verse is one that pastors often use at the end of the church service- 2 Corinthians 13:14, "May the grace of the Lord Jesus Christ, and the love of God, and the communion of the Holy Ghost be with you all." This verse helps us to know that the Holy Spirit is with us so that we can talk to God and know what He wants us to do. We can have fellowship, or an all-the-time friendship with God.

How the wind reminds me of the Holy Spirit

1. it is powerful
2. it changes things
3. we can't see it but we can see what it does

Through-the-Week Mystery Message

On a windy day this week take time to sit and watch the wind. See if you can think of some ways the wind reminds you of the Holy Spirit. Write them on this blue circle.

Suggested answers: (1) It is powerful. (2) It changes things. (3) We can't see it but we can see what it does.

Provide an approximately 5" circle of blue construction paper with the words "How the wind reminds me of the Holy Spirit" around the top edge. Offer a small prize for each one who brings the circle back with at least one fact on it. Share facts.

– E.L.

Do you ever wonder about the third Person of the Trinity— the Holy Spirit?

Here's a song you can learn to teach you who the Holy Spirit is.

(Sing to tune of "Away in a Manger")

My friend Holy Spirit I
sure cannot see,
But He is from God
And He's comforting me.
He helps me to know what
is true and what's not.
He's part of the Trinity and
loves me lots!

My friend Holy Spirit is
with me each hour.
It says in the Bible He
fills me with power.
As I try to follow the
Bible so true,
The Spirit of God helps
me know what to do!

Read 1 Corinthians 2:12, John 15:26 and Acts 1:5-8. Underline all the words in the song that you find in these verses. Use a red and black crayon to fill in the shapes below and discover one more thing the Spirit of God will do for the Christian.

Red = ● ●
Black = ●

He is my:

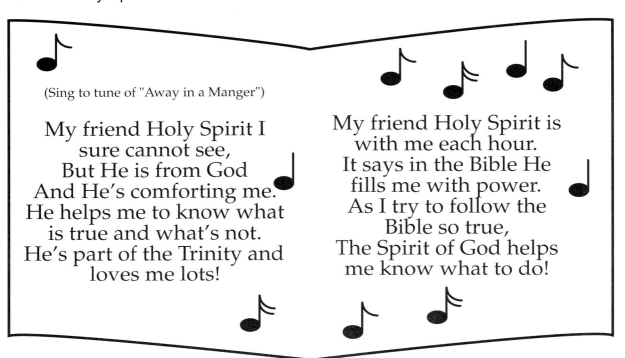

John 16:13 gives the answer!

Sin is disobeying God.
All have sinned.

Object: Empty pencil box with lid

There's something in this box God wants you to think about.

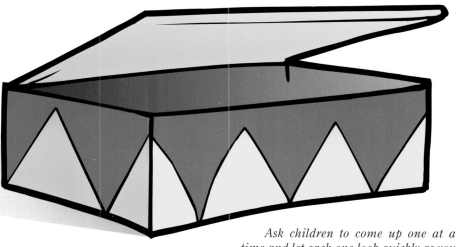

Ask children to come up one at a time and let each one look quickly as you hold the lid open. Tell them to keep it a secret until everyone has looked.

What is in the box? *(The children will no doubt say nothing.)*

Nothing?

(Close the lid.) But it's in there now. *(Open it.)* Now it's not there. *(Repeat several times until someone guesses, or tell them.)*

It is *darkness!*

When I open the lid the darkness is gone because the light has entered. There cannot be darkness and light at the same time.

Darkness reminds me of something God calls *sin.* Sin is disobeying God. It is not following His rules. Every person in the world has sinned. The Bible tells us, "All have sinned" (Romans 3:23) and "The wages of sin is death"—separation from God forever and ever (Romans 6:23).

The Bible also tells us, "God is light, and in him is no darkness at all" (1 John 1:5). So we cannot be where He is.

We need someone to take away our darkness of sin. The Lord Jesus, God's own perfect Son, said, "I am the light of the world: he that followeth me shall not walk in darkness, but shall have the light of life" (John 8:12).

We can thank the Lord for the wonderful light He has brought into our lives. We need to pray for the many, many people who are still in darkness.

Through-the-Week Mystery Message

Close your eyes tight and think about darkness for a few minutes. What are some things you don't like about darkness? Write these on this gray piece of paper and bring it back to class next week.

(1) It can be scary. (2) I can't see the beautiful things God has made. (3) Sometimes people do bad things in the dark. (4) I can't see where I'm going. (5) I feel alone.

Provide a ragged piece of gray paper for each child to write on. Offer a small prize for each one who brings theirs back. Next week review John 8:12 and have the children tear up the gray sheet to remind them that Jesus takes away our sins and our fears. He shows us the way to live and helps us see the many beautiful things God wants to do for us.

–M.E

Craft 4

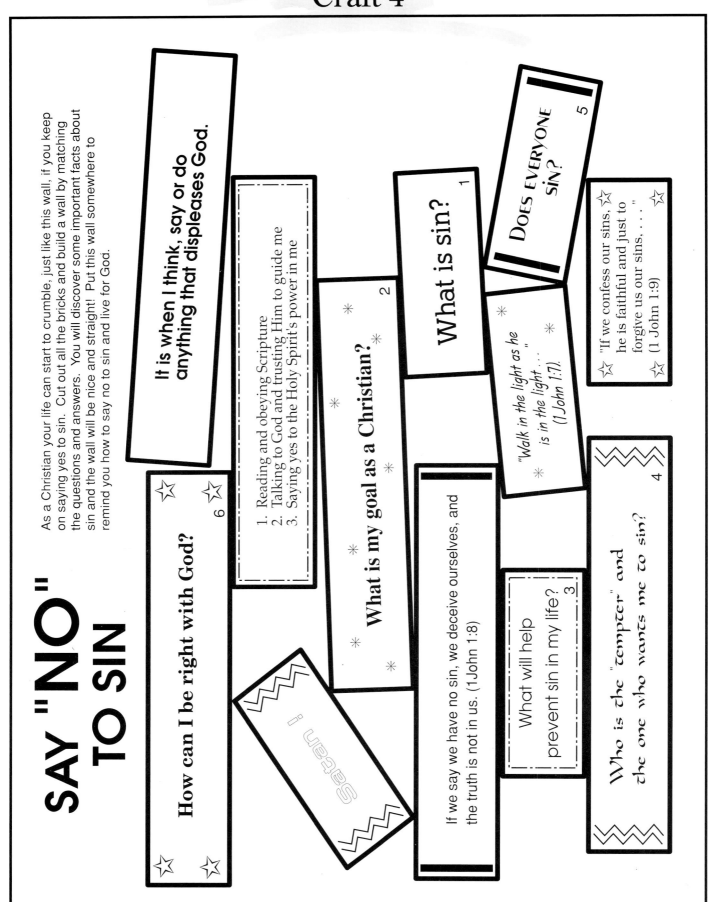

SAY "NO" TO SIN

As a Christian your life can start to crumble, just like this wall, if you keep on saying yes to sin. Cut out all the bricks and build a wall by matching the questions and answers. You will discover some important facts about sin and the wall will be nice and straight! Put this wall somewhere to remind you how to say no to sin and live for God.

It is when I think, say or do anything that displeases God.

Does EVERYONE sin?

5

What is sin?

1

"If we confess our sins, he is faithful and just to forgive us our sins, . . ." (1 John 1:9)

2

What is my goal as a Christian?

"Walk in the light as he is in the light . . . ." (1 John 1:7).

How can I be right with God?

6

1. Reading and obeying Scripture
2. Talking to God and trusting Him to guide me
3. Saying yes to the Holy Spirit's power in me

If we say we have no sin, we deceive ourselves, and the truth is not in us. (1 John 1:8)

What will help prevent sin in my life?

3

Who is the "tempter" and the one who wants me to sin?

4

Satan!

Jesus died and rose again for the sins of all the world.

Objects: United States history book and the Bible

How do we know George Washington was a real man who lived many, many years ago? Yes. People have written about him in books. *(Read a few statements from the history book.)* What do we call things that happened long ago? *(History.)* You will have many history books to read as you study in school.

(Show a Bible.) Did you know that this book is a history book? The Bible is God's history book. It is history because the things we read in it really happened. But the Bible is much more than that. It is God's own words to us. It's His way of talking to you and me. Where do you think you would learn about the history of Jesus, God's Son—in the United States history book or the Bible? Right.

Let's look at some very important facts about Jesus who lived on this earth long before George Washington. Here in 1 Corinthians 15:3,4 we read, " . . . Christ died for our sins according to the Scriptures, and that he was buried, and that he rose again on the third day according to the Scriptures . . . . " (Scriptures is another name for the Bible.)

God's own perfect Son came to earth to die for our sins and rise again. This is the most important thing that ever happened in history. The Bible goes on to tell us that over 500 people saw Jesus after He rose from the dead (1 Cor. 15:6). We can know for sure that He not only died for our sins but that He conquered death!

Through-the-Week Mystery Message

This week I'd like you to draw or write a history book about you! Tell when you were born, some of the important things that have happened in your life and the most important event—about when you believed Jesus died and rose again for *your* sins!

Provide a small booklet of stapled pages and a construction paper cover for each child. Offer a small prize for the three best books. —E. L.

Craft 5

Here's a fun way to tell your family and pals about an important fact:

Jesus died and rose again for the sins of all the world!

Do a Puppet Poem

No. 1: Did you know that Jesus
(you died and that He rose again?
puppet) Did you know He suffered
much to cover up my sin?
Did you know that Jesus died
not only just for me?

No. 2: Did you know He also died
for kids across the sea?

No. 3: Did you know that even folks
who've lived a long, long while
Need this same forgiving

No. 4: love just like a little child?
Did you know that this good
news is written in God's Book?

All: Did you know it's there for
all and you can take a look!

4.

3.

A. Color the finger puppets. Trace one and draw *you* on it (puppet no. 1).
B. Cut out puppets and fold.
C. Glue along top and sides. Let dry!
D. Practice reading the poem.
E. Put your puppets on your fingers. (You may need two fingers in each.)
F. Find a friend or mom or brother and DO A PUPPET POEM! Wiggle the puppets at the appropriate times!

Check out 1 Corinthians 15:3, 4 and Romans 5:8

2.

We are saved from our sins by believing on the Lord Jesus Christ and receiving Him as our Savior.

Object: Life preserver (white ring) or a white Life Saver®

I brought each of you a piece of candy to enjoy as I'm talking. *(Give each child one white Life Saver.)*

Hold up life preserver or white Life Saver. Begin with the appropriate question: "Do you know what this white ring is used for?" or "Do you know what this Life Saver reminds me of?" Follow with a discussion of its use.

A life preserver can save a person who is drowning. It can be tossed to the person who can grab hold of it and be pulled to safety. Did you know the candy you are enjoying was made to look like a life preserver? In fact it is called what? *(A Life Saver.)*

In order for a person to be saved from drowning he has to believe the life preserver will save him, then he has to reach out and receive it—just like you reached out to receive the Life Saver candy.

This is a picture of what you did when you were saved from your sin. God sent His Son, the Lord Jesus Christ, to save you from the punishment of sin by dying on the cross. But you needed to believe that Jesus did that for you and receive Him as your very own Savior. How did you receive Him? By asking Him to forgive your sin and give you everlasting life. You have God's promise in John 3:16. *(Have children say verse together.)*

Many people think they can be saved from sin in other ways. But God tells us in the Bible in Jesus' own words, "No man cometh unto the Father, but by me" (John 14:6). Jesus is your life saver!

Through-the-Week Mystery Message

Our wonderful Creator God has good plans for us. He planned for us to have everlasting life through His Son. He also planned life for our bodies here on earth. See if you can think of some things this week that you need to receive for your body to live. Write them on this life preserver and bring it back to class. *(Answers should include: water, food, air.)*

Make a 5" x 5" white posterboard life preserver for each child to take home. Next week point out the parallel between one way for our bodies to live—by receiving nourishment—and one way for our spirits to live—by receiving Christ. People must choose God's way to live! —L.S.

Craft 6

JESUS IS
THE ONLY WAY TO GOD!

Do you like mazes? How many right paths get you to the end?_____
In John 14:6 Jesus says, "I am the way, the truth, and the life: no man cometh unto the Father, but by me."

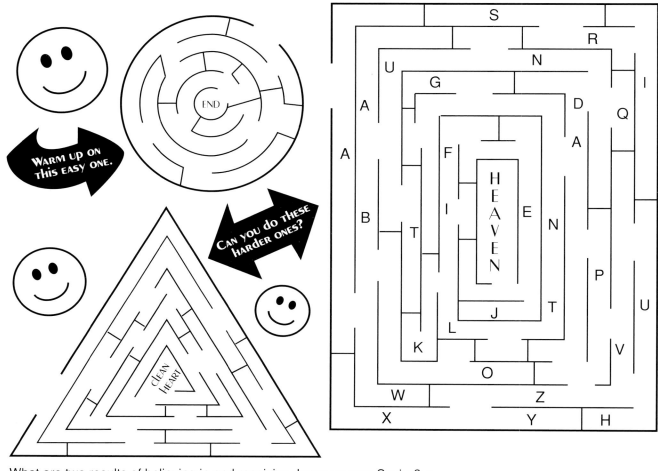

WARM UP ON THIS EASY ONE.

CAN YOU DO THESE HARDER ONES?

END

CLEAN HEART

HEAVEN

What are two results of believing in and receiving Jesus as your Savior? a _____
_____ and _____. (Hint: Check middle of triangle and rectangle!)

CAN YOU FINISH THIS VERSE?

For God so loved the world, that he gave his only begotten Son, That

_____

_____ John 3:16.

Bonus "mystery." Results of being a Christian. (Start at beginning of rectangular maze path. Put letters in blanks.)

___ ___ ___ ___ ___ ___ ___   ___ ___ ___ ___

When we receive Christ His Holy Spirit comes to live in us and we belong to God forever.

Objects: A clear glass bowl containing water and several little sponges (Have a paper towel to dry your hand.)

We will let the water in this bowl remind us of the Lord Jesus. Each of these sponges stands for a person who has received Him as his Savior. *(Put sponges into water so they are fully saturated.)* When you receive the Lord Jesus as your Savior from sin the Bible says you are "in Christ" (Col. 1:2, 28). You will be in His family forever.

But not only are you in Christ, He is in you by His Holy Spirit. These sponges are filled with the water, aren't they? They are in the water and the water is in them. You are in Christ and Christ is in you.

The Bible says that because you are God's child He sent the Spirit of His Son to live in your heart (Gal. 4:6). God's Holy Spirit in you is God's promise that you belong to Him (Eph. 1:13-14).

We have learned that the Father, Son and Holy Spirit are our three-in-one God. So we know that the Holy Spirit is all-powerful. No one can take Him out of your life—not even you! In the Bible you are guaranteed that some day you will be with God. His Holy Spirit in you is that guarantee.

To be in Christ and to have Christ in you is a wonderful mystery. You can see that the sponges are in the water and you can see that the water is in the sponges. *(Hold sponge above bowl and squeeze a little out.)* But you cannot see the Lord. So how do you know you are in Him and He is in you? *(Let children give answers.)* Yes, God has told us in His Word and His promises never fail!

Through-the-Week Mystery Message

Be a detective this week and keep a list of evidence that shows the Holy Spirit is living in your heart. These are some "clues" from the Bible that will help you: The Holy Spirit speaks to you as you read the Bible, tells you when you are doing something wrong, helps you to do hard things and make right decisions, comforts you when you are sad, changes you so that you become more like Jesus. *(Give children some examples from your life.)*

Provide a little black book (several pages of typing paper, folded with construction paper cover and stapled) and a small pencil for each child to record his evidence. List the Bible clues above on the first page so they will remember what to look for. Let children share their evidence the following week. Offer an incentive if desired.

—M.E.

There is a friend who *sticks* closer than a brother . . .

When Jesus is our Savior His Holy Spirit comes to live in us and God sticks with us permanently. Read Ephesians 1:13b–14.

It's

JESUS!

(through His Holy Spirit)

Here are two "sticky" projects to do with an adult friend or parent. Read the Bible verse when your project is completed! How about sharing them with your friend or parent too?

"STICKY" GLOB

Put 1 tablespoon of liquid starch into a bowl. Add 1 tablespoon of white glue. Mix starch over and over into glue . . . press, push and pull until it's not sticky--about 5 minutes. Be patient. Surprise! It bounces and stretches.
For color add 3 drops of food coloring. **Proverbs 18:24**

"STICKY" STRING

Float an ice cube in a full glass of water. Lay a wet string across the top of ice cube. Sprinkle salt on string and ice cube. Count to 40. Pull on string. What happens? **Hebrews 13:5b**

Permanent Glue

Object Lesson 8

**Object: Bar of soap
(You will also need a pan
of water, cloth towel and a
piece of charcoal.)**

(Have several smudges from charcoal on your face before you begin.)

What would you think if I told you I have an appointment to visit the President of the United States today? You would think I'd better use this soap real quick, wouldn't you? *(Wash off the smudges.)*

Do we have to make an appointment to visit God? No. He is with us all the time. I'm sure He doesn't like to see us walking around with dirty faces. But there is something much worse than that. God does not like sin in our hearts. In fact, the Bible says God hates sin (Prov. 6:16-19). God hates sin so much He sent His own Son to die so that He could cleanse us from sin.

Let's say that I had a fight with a friend today and called her some really bad things. Am I ever glad for this bar of soap. I'll just wash away those bad words.

(Wash lips.) Oh yes, and I took a pen from someone and decided not to return it. I better wash the hand that took it. *(Wash hand.)* And I thought something very unkind about the person who won a prize at the store yesterday because I wanted to win it. I better wash away that bad thought. *(Wash forehead.)*

Can I really wash away bad words and actions and thoughts? Of course not! Well, then how can I ever have the clean life God wants me to have? I know Jesus forgave my sin when I received Him as my Savior. But what about those sins I've done since then?

Did you know that God never asks us to do something without making a way? He has said He wants us to live holy lives—not to let sin stay in our hearts. He is the one who is able to cleanse us from all sin. Here are His instructions: "If we confess our sins, he is faithful and just to forgive us our sins, and to cleanse us from all unrighteousness" (1 John 1:9).

If you tell the Lord you have sinned and you are sorry for that sin, He is only too glad to forgive you. He hates sin and does not want it to hurt your friendship with Him.

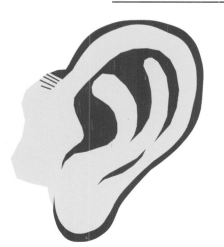

**Through-the-Week
Mystery Message**

As you take a bath or shower this week think about the clean life inside that God wants you to have. As you wash your ears, think if you have listened to any dirty stories. Face—did you look at anything that wouldn't please God? Did you say any mean or wrong words? Hands—did you do anything that God has commanded you not to? Feet—did you go anywhere you were not supposed to go? Head—did you think any bad thoughts? You can tell (confess) any sins to God right there. As you rinse off the soap, thank Him for His wonderful promise to clean you from all your sin!

(Give the children an opportunity to praise the Lord for His forgiveness in your next meeting.) —M.E.

God Hates Sin!

He wants you to live a clean life!

How? After you receive Jesus as your Savior let Him be Lord of your life. You can do these things written on the bars of soap:

If we confess our sins, he is faithful and just to forgive us our sins, and to cleanse us from all unrighteousness.
1 John 1:9

Wherewithal shall a young man cleanse his way? By taking heed thereto according to thy word.
Psalm 119:9

Finally, brethren, whatsoever things are true, . . . honest . . . just . . . pure . . . lovely . . . think on these things.
Philippians 4:8

Thy word have I hid in mine heart, that I might not sin against thee.
Psalm 119:11

Blessed is the man that walketh not in the counsel of the ungodly, nor standeth in the way of sinners, nor sitteth in the seat of the scornful.
Psalm 1:1

Submit yourselves therefore to God. Resist the devil, and he will flee from you.
James 4:7

Cut the "bars" out. Put them in the bottom of a dish soap bottle as a reminder to stay "clean" in your heart.

God has a plan for our life and gives us the power to follow that plan.

Object: Digital watch

Who can tell me how to set the time on this watch? *(If a child doesn't know, explain how it works.)* What if I decide to hit this button twice instead of once and not hold the second button down? *(Make question conflict with explanation of how the watch should work.)*

Who decided that the watch should work this way? *(The one who made it.)* Right! The person who designed this watch had a plan to make it work just right and do the job it was made for.

The almighty God of Heaven and earth made you. He has a plan for your life and wants you to follow that plan each day. Listen to this exciting verse from God's Word: "We are his workmanship, created in Christ Jesus unto good works, which God hath before ordained . . ." (Ephesians 2:10).

How does God show you His plan? He speaks to your heart as you read His instruction book, the Bible, and talk to Him in prayer. His Holy Spirit guides you throughout each day.

What happens if you decide to do things a different way than God's plan? *(You will not be able to do the special job God has made you to do.)* You will miss out on God's purpose for your life.

Let's think about this watch again. Suppose I push all the right buttons the right number of times. Do the buttons work on their own? What gives them power to change the watch's time? *(The battery.)*

Who gives you the power to obey God? *(The Holy Spirit who lives inside of you!)* What a wonderful God you have. He shows you His plan for your life and gives you all the power you need to follow it!

Through-the-Week Mystery Message

Just as God planned so perfectly the number of minutes in a day, He has a perfect plan for your life. He knows how long your life will be. He tells us in the Bible to "redeem the time." That means, make it count for good! Do you think you could do 12 good things this week—one for each number on the clock? How will you know what to do? Ask God! Read the Bible! Listen to the Holy Spirit! Here is a clock with 12 slips in. Each time you do something good write it on a slip. Next week we will see how many good works we have done that God planned for us to do even before we were born.

Make a clock face approximately 5″ in diameter for each child. Cut a plain circle the same size and glue around bottom and sides to make a pocket. Insert 12 slips of paper, approximately 5″ x 1″. Have a praise time the following week as the children share how God has used them.

—E. L.

Craft 9

God Has a Plan

1 **HERE IS A PILE OF ODDS AND ENDS:**

Your life was kind of like that pile before you received Jesus as your Savior.

But . . . .

2 **PUT THE ODDS AND ENDS TOGETHER, AS THESE PICTURE "PLANS" SHOW, TO MAKE 3 NEAT TOYS!**

You need the "plans," don't you?
It's just like that with God. He has a wonderful plan for your life and gives you the power to follow the plan! (Philippians 4:13)

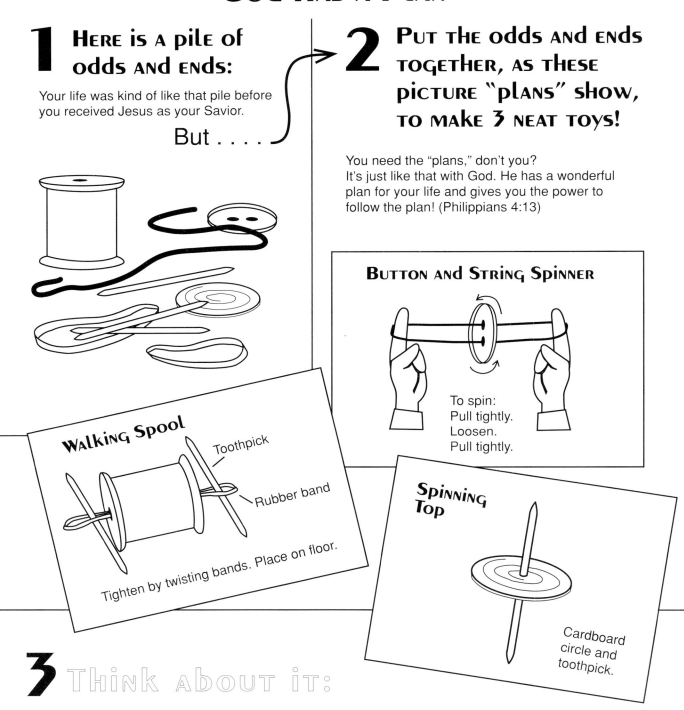

BUTTON AND STRING SPINNER

To spin:
Pull tightly.
Loosen.
Pull tightly.

WALKING SPOOL

Toothpick

Rubber band

Tighten by twisting bands. Place on floor.

SPINNING TOP

Cardboard circle and toothpick.

3 **Think about it:**

A. You were made by God and He has a special job for you to do. (See Ephesians 2:10.)
B. Are you following God's plan for your life?
C. Are you looking for that plan as you read the Bible each day?
D. Can you show these toys to a friend and tell him about God's great plan for those who believe in Him?

A Christian no longer belongs to himself; he lives for God.

Object: Cut a 9" x 12" cross from construction paper. Fold top section behind, then fold left and right sections behind.

Before you received Christ you took charge of your own life. *(Hold up folded cross to represent "I".)* You may have thought, *I will laugh at that kid—he's dumb,* or *I will look at that video at my friend's house, even though Mom wouldn't like it.*

But now that Jesus lives in your heart He is in charge of your life. He wants you to please Him in all you do. One way to please the Lord is to reach out to others with His love. *(Unfold left and right sections of cross.)* You can show them God's love by helping with a problem or need they have. You can tell them how much God loves them by sharing a great verse from the Bible, like John 3:16.

The most important part of living for God is to let Him take charge of your life. *(Unfold top section of cross.)* Look up to God and ask Him what He wants you to do. The Bible says, "You are not your own; you were bought with a price" (1 Cor. 6:19-20). What is the price that was paid to set you free from sin? Yes, God's own Son died on the cross for you. Your life is no longer yours. It belongs to God.

When you ask God what He wants you to do before you laugh at someone or before you look at a bad video, what do you think His answer will be? When you ask God if you should give part of your allowance to help those who are hungry or if you should invite someone to Sunday school, I wonder what He will say?

Here's something special you need to know: whatever God asks you to do, He will help you do it. It is exciting to live for God!

1

2

3

Through-the-Week Mystery Message

Here is a fold-up cross to take home. When you do something to reach out and share God's love with someone open one side section. When you share God's love again open

the second side section. When you think about doing something unkind or that doesn't please Mom or Dad, pray and ask God to help you do the right thing. Then lift up the top of the cross. After all three parts are open, turn your cross over and read the mystery message. If you do not peek before the cross is open, tell me next week and I will give you ..." (a small award in a cross shape if available).

(Make a folded cross for each child from one-half sheet construction paper. Print GOD SEES ALL YOU DO! Prov. 15:3 in section covered by folded parts.)

—E. L.

I belong to Jesus

When you start your day do you think about who you belong to?

Try this:
1. Read 1 Corinthians 6:19-20
2. Memorize 2 Corinthians 5:15
3. Complete the art project below and put it near your bed on a table as a reminder to live for God.

What would Jesus do?

I belong to Him!

★ ★

1

3-D reminder

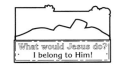

What would Jesus do?
I belong to Him!

1. Color all three panels in bright colors.
2. Cut along outside edges.
3. Staple, tape or glue the panels together at each end by stacking the stars on top of each other in order-- number one on top. (Staples will work best.)
4. It should look like this from the top.

2 Corinthians 5:15

★ ★

2

★ ★

3

Satan is the enemy of God but God is all powerful.

Object: A plastic snake

(Pull snake out of box or from behind something in a way that will cause children to react.)

Yuk! That's just what I wanted you to say! A snake is usually something we run from. Another word for *snake* is *serpent*. Do you remember where we first read about a snake in the Bible? Yes, in the very first story, in Genesis 3. God's enemy, Satan, appeared as a serpent. He tempted the first man and woman to do wrong and he has been doing that ever since. Satan wants to destroy people for he knows how much God loves us. Satan is God's enemy and ours, too.

Some snakes are very powerful. (A python can kill an animal weighing 100 pounds.) Satan is powerful. He is more powerful than you and I. Snakes slither through the grass and often people don't realize they are nearby until they attack. Satan tries to trick us into doing wrong. If we are not careful, we will do what he wants before we realize it.

How can we escape this enemy who wants to ruin our lives? We know someone who is much more powerful than Satan. Who is that? *(God.)* And where does He live? *(In our hearts.)* Yes, He lives in you by His Holy Spirit. Listen to this great promise—"Greater is he that is in you than he that is in the world" (1 John 4:4). Jesus lives in you to give you power over Satan who is in the world. The Lord Jesus will give you His power as you call on Him and trust Him. What a wonderful God we have! He will not let our enemy destroy us.

Through-the-Week Mystery Message

Jesus is our protection against Satan. Here is a Bible search you can do this week to find out how Jesus protects you. Look in Ephesians 6:10-18 for the answers. Bring your chart back with the answers written in next week. *(Teacher: Encourage full participation by offering a small reward. Take time to discuss each part of God's armor with the children during that session.)*

Make copies of the Christian soldier and prepare a chart for each child, providing a blank line beside each piece of armor. Print Ephesians 6:10 at top of chart. Add this line at bottom: And don't forget to ___ ___ ___ ___!   —*E.L.*

See Satan Run!

Do you know the Bible tells us God is more powerful than Satan? Here's how God will give you victory over Satan's temptations!

★ Let Jesus take charge of your life. (submit)
★ Read and obey the Bible. (submit)
★ Pray and ask for God's strength to say NO to Satan. (resist)

Then, guess what? Satan "will pull on his track shoes" and run (flee) from you because you are letting God take charge!

Cut out the square below. Color the track shoe. Cut around the shoe on dotted lines only. (Not the bottom.) Fold shoe up at the bottom. Set this shoe somewhere so you're reminded that Satan will run when you submit to God.

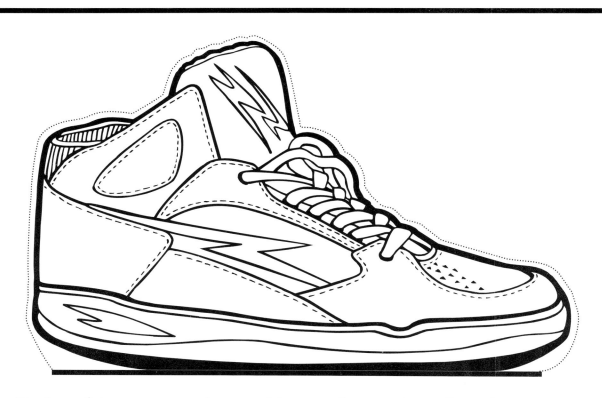

Submit yourselves therefore to God.
Resist the devil, and he will **flee** from you.

James 4:7

The Bible is God's holy Word to help us live for Him.

Object: A good size mirror and a Bible; a piece of charcoal

(Hold up the mirror and Bible.) I have a riddle for you today. How many mirrors do I have in my hands? *(One.)* No, I have two mirrors! Can you figure out the answer to this riddle? Yes, the Bible is like a mirror. Let's find out how.

(Hold up mirror and have a child look into it with his back to the class. Hold mirror on an angle which enables them to see his face.) Can you see John's face? *(Yes.)* No, you can't really see John's face, but you can see what it looks like because of the mirror.

No one has ever seen God. But when you look into the Bible you will read many wonderful things about God. You will see what He is like.

God is holy—perfectly good. God, who is holy, gave us the Bible and it is perfectly good. In 2 Timothy 3:16 we read, "All Scripture [another name for the Bible] is given by inspiration of God, and is profitable [useful] for doctrine, for reproof, for correction, for instruction in righteousness [right living]." All those words add up to one thing—the Bible shows us how to live for God.

(Add black streak to your face with charcoal.) How do I know when I have dirt on my face? I look in the mirror and see it. What does that tell me? I need to wash my face. When we read the Bible it not only tells us the things God wants us to do, it shows us our sin and helps us to change. God's Word is not like any other book. It has power to help us stop sinning and please God.

Through-the-Week Mystery Message

In this envelope are five things God has asked us to do in His holy book, the Bible. Each day pull out one slip and hold it up to a mirror. Ask God to help you do it for Him that day. Tell us about one of the things you did in class next week and we will praise the Lord together for His wonderful guidebook for our lives!

On one sheet of paper print five commands backwards from the following verses: Eph. 6:1; Eph. 4:25; Eph. 4:32; James 1:4; 1 John 4:7. Make a photo copy for each child. Cut apart each command and place each set in an envelope with question marks or stickers on the front.

—*E. L.*

Craft 12

GOD'S WORD
Is A Daily Guide On The
ROAD OF LIFE!

1. Find each sad face and circle the word near it that makes God unhappy (and makes you unhappy, too!)
2. Look up the Bible verse in the nearby sign to discover some advice or good news from God's Word.
3. Color in the sign if you believe the words in the Bible verse can guide your life!

Peace Pass
Phil. 4:7

Bully Brook

Mumblers' Mountains

Buddy Bridge
Prov. 17:17

Chaos Crossroad

Frustration Forest

Level-
headed Lane
1 Cor. 14:40

N
W — E
S

Happy Hut
Prov. 16:20

Truth Trail
Eph 4:15

Tattletail
Tracks

Busy Beach
Prov. 6:6-8

Lazy Lake

All Scripture is given by inspiration of God and is profitable for doctrine, for reproof, for correction, for instruction in righteousness.
2 Timothy 3:16

God hears and answers our prayers.

Object: A toy or real telephone that is not connected

Did you ever wish you could call God on the telephone? Suppose you had a telephone number for Heaven. How would you go about calling God? First you would have to dial the number. What do you think His number might be? *(Let children think a while. A suggestion could be 123-7777. "123" because of the Trinity. "7777" because "7" is the number God uses many times in the Bible to carry out His plans.)*

(Pretend to dial the number.) Oops, the line is busy! *(Dial again.)* Still busy. But I need to talk to God now. I'll try once more. *(Dial again.)* Hello. Hello. Oh there's a lot of noise on this line. I sure wish there were a better way to talk to God. This is frustrating.

Well, we've been just pretending. There is a better way to talk to God, isn't there? What wonderful, special, awesome way is that? *(Prayer.)*

God has planned this way for His children. No busy signals, no static, no dialing or even waiting one single second. God hears our prayers instantly. Because He is so great He can listen to the prayers of His children anytime, anywhere. He can even listen to all our prayers at the same time!

If God had a telephone number His area code might be thirty-three three. Those numbers remind us of the promise He has given us in the book of Jeremiah. In Jeremiah 33:3 God says, "Call unto me and I will answer you."

How does God answer us? *(By His Holy Spirit in our heart, through the Bible, through other Christians.)*

Aren't you glad you don't have to look for a telephone every time you want to talk to God?

Through-the-Week Mystery Message

This week I'd like you to think again about how much better prayer is than having to telephone God. *(Show coiled paper.)* Let this paper remind you of a telephone cord. It doesn't reach very far, does it? But, remember, prayer can reach *anywhere!* I'd like you to talk to God in many different places this week. Write down each place you pray on this strip of paper. Someone else can write down what you tell them if you cannot write. Bring your rolled up paper to class next time and we will share some of the places we have prayed. If you pray in at least seven different places you will receive a prize. *(Teacher, try to award something related to prayer.)*

For each child, prepare a coiled paper to represent a telephone cord. Cut three 1" x 11" strips of paper and tape them together. Roll tightly around a pencil. When the paper is slid off the end and unwound it will give a coiled effect. Reroll the paper and band it for easy carrying.

—E.L.

Craft 13

No Busy Signals

God **never** puts you on hold!

God is **always** there in prayer!

1. Cut out head, eyes and slits.
2. Cut out four strips below.
3. Tape top two strips at dotted lines. Tape bottom two strips at dotted lines.
4. Insert strips in slits and pull through eyes and mouth to show various feelings.

How about sharing this with a sad friend! It will help him!

No matter how you feel or where you are God **ALWAYS** *hears* and *answers* your prayer!

check out Jeremiah 33:3.

slit   cut out   cut out   slit

← carefully cut these slits →

Jesus is preparing a place for us in Heaven so that we can live with Him forever.

Object: Prepare a sign from yellow or orange posterboard that reads CONSTRUCTION AHEAD. Print DETOUR on the back.

Sometimes as you are traveling in a car you will see the sign "Construction Ahead." What does this mean? *(It often means someone is hard at work building something new.)*

Before Jesus died on the cross, rose again and returned to Heaven, He left us with a fantastic promise! He said there would be "construction ahead." Someone would be building a place for us to live forever. Do you know who that person is? The Lord Jesus Himself! Listen to His own words in John 14:3: "I go to prepare a place for you." This promise is for all those who have trusted Him as their Savior.

Jesus is busy right now getting Heaven ready for you. God tells us there will be no more death or crying or pain in that wonderful place (Rev. 21:3). Because there is no sin there Heaven will be absolutely perfect! There will be many rooms (John 14:2)—rooms for all who belong to the Lord Jesus. No one will be crowded into a tiny place. No one will have to sleep on the street!

What is another sign that you sometimes see after "Construction Ahead"? *(Detour.)* Did you ever get lost by taking a detour? I have! That's why I'm especially glad for the second part of Jesus' promise: "And if I go and prepare a place for you, I will come back and take you to be with me ...." No detours on the way to Heaven. Jesus Himself will come to take us straight to His heavenly home. And we will be with the Lord *forever* (1 Thess. 4:17)!

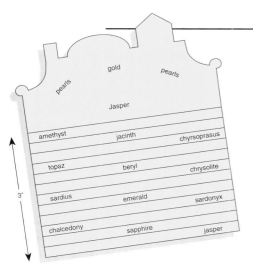

Through-the-Week Mystery Message

In Revelation, the last book in the Bible, God tells us about some of the materials that are being used to build the City of Heaven. This week look up Revelation chapter 21, verses 15 to 21 and print all the things you find that will be part of this city. Print them on this silhouette at the correct location. If there are some jewels you have never heard of you might look them up in the dictionary to see what color they are. Print the color after the name of the jewel or draw and color a jewel. Bring the silhouette of Heaven back next week and we will talk more about this wonderful place which will be our home forever.

Make a simple Heaven silhouette with a 3″ foundation for each child. Cut from bright yellow or orange construction paper. Divide the foundation into 12 quarter-inch sections. Print Revelation 21:15 to 21 with instructions on back of silhouette. The items they should find are: gold, jasper (mostly green), sapphire (mostly deep blue), chalcedony (pale blue or gray), emerald (green), sardonyx (deep orange red), sardius (red), chrysolite (green), beryl (green, yellow, pink or white), topaz (yellow), chrysoprasus (apple green), jacinth (orange), amethyst (purple), pearls. You may be able to find pictures of these jewels in a large dictionary or encyclopedia to show the children. Offer a small prize for each one who brings his silhouette with some work done on it. A bonus may be given to those who list 10 or more. Take time to thank the Lord for preparing Heaven for us. —*E. L.*

Craft 14

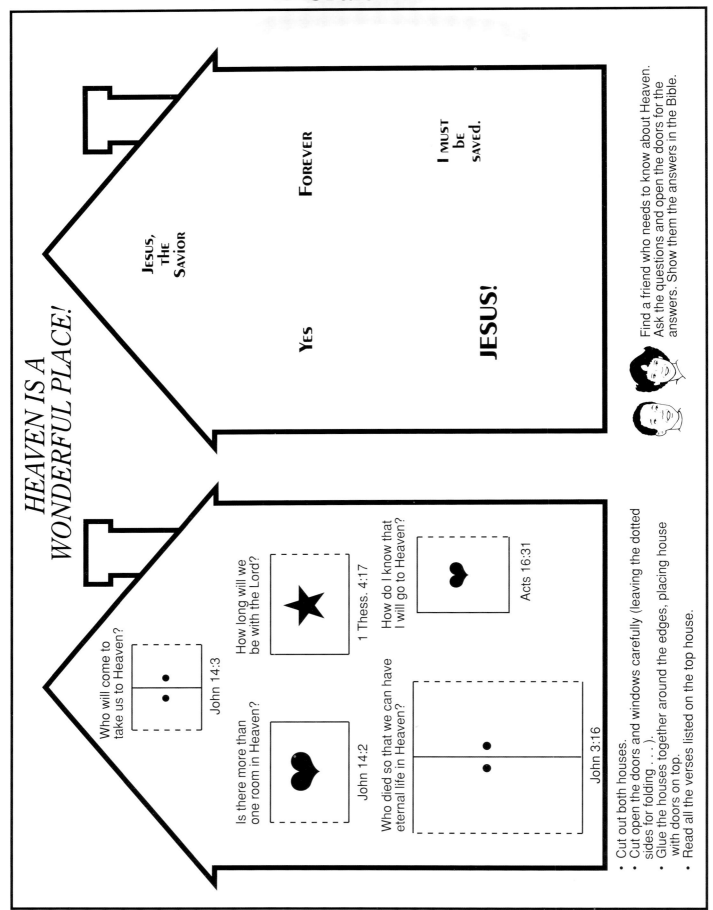

HEAVEN IS A WONDERFUL PLACE!

JESUS, THE SAVIOR

FOREVER

I MUST BE SAVED.

YES

JESUS!

Find a friend who needs to know about Heaven. Ask the questions and open the doors for the answers. Show them the answers in the Bible.

Who will come to take us to Heaven?

John 14:3

How long will we be with the Lord?

1 Thess. 4:17

How do I know that I will go to Heaven?

Acts 16:31

Is there more than one room in Heaven?

John 14:2

Who died so that we can have eternal life in Heaven?

John 3:16

- Cut out both houses.
- Cut open the doors and windows carefully (leaving the dotted sides for folding . . . .).
- Glue the houses together around the edges, placing house with doors on top.
- Read all the verses listed on the top house.

I BELIEVE
(A Creed for Children)

Cynthia L. McClurg

C. L. M.

How to Lead a Child to Christ

1. Show him his NEED of salvation; that all persons are not going to Heaven; that no one in himself is good enough to go and the result of sin is forever separation from God (Romans 3:23; Revelation 21:27; John 8:21,24).

2. Show him the WAY of salvation. Salvation is a free gift because the Lord Jesus took our place on the cross, was buried and rose again from the dead (John 3:16; Ephesians 2:8; 1 Corinthians 15:3, 4).

3. Lead him to RECEIVE the gift of salvation, even Jesus Christ, by trusting Him as his personal Savior (John 1:12; Revelation 3:20).

4. From the Word of God, help him find ASSURANCE of his salvation (John 3:36; Revelation 3:20; Hebrews 13:5).

5. Lead him to CONFESS Christ (Matthew 10:32). This confession should be made to you, other workers, later to his friends and as circumstances permit, in a public church service.

I Believe
Visualized Teaching Tool and Song

A fun way for a Christian child to commit his beliefs to memory through symbols, song and a small take-home booklet! Beautifully illustrated 11 x 16 ½" book with teaching text, exciting review games, music and reproducible pages.

Order from your Christian bookstore, local CEF or CEF Press, Box 348, Warrenton, MO 63383-0348.

CEF PRESS®
A ministry of Child Evangelism Fellowship® Inc.

Helping You Evangelize Children

WARRENTON, MO 63383-0348

03-C030-001

Christian Belief £5.00
Object Lesson

ISBN 1-55976-165-2